Europe

Israel

Asia

Australia

Translated by: Yael Mermelstein

Photography: Israel Bardugo

Layout and Design:
Boaz Sharon - www.keysharon.co.il

Special thanks to Motti Feigelstock and family

Published by Menucha Publishers Inc.
250 44th Street, Brooklyn, NY 11232
Tel/Fax: 718-232-0856
1855-Menucha | www.menuchapublishers.com
ISBN: 978161465174-1

Motti of Paraguay

Young Lamplighters

by **Ella Verzov** • **Chana Oirechman**
Translated by **Yael Mermelstein**

Hi, there. My name is Motti and I live in Asunción, the capital of Paraguay. I can't wait to tell you all about this interesting South American country, but first, let me tell you a little bit about me.

4

You'll never guess what kind of alarm clock I have. No matter how early I wake up in the morning, there's always someone up earlier than me. Well, not exactly someone. I have a chicken coop in my backyard! I wake up every morning to the sounds of the birds chirping in the trees that surround my yard, and of course to the sound of the rooster — *cock-a-doodle-doo!*

Guess who takes care of the chickens? Me! I make sure they have enough food and water, that they're protected from the rain and the sun, and that there are no animals around that might bother them. I can even understand chicken language. I know when their sounds mean, "I'm hungry," and when their sounds mean, "I'm sad."

I make sure to spread seeds on the ground for my chickens to eat before I eat my own breakfast. It's a mitzvah to feed your animals before you feed yourself!

Morning in
our backyard

A few weeks ago, I went outside to feed the chickens when I saw something white sticking out of a crack in the ground. It was an egg! I ran and called my four sisters to come look, and my mother followed, too.

"Mommy, can we make an omelet?" my four-year-old sister, Blumy, asked.

"We can make an omelet with the eggs we buy from the grocery store," my mother said. "But we can't touch this egg. In the next few weeks the hen will lay more eggs. Then she'll sit on them for a few more weeks and then — the eggs will hatch into baby chicks! You just have to be patient."

And that's exactly what happened. The hen laid another egg every day. Only when she'd laid twelve eggs did she finally sit on her eggs.

Have you ever seen a hen sitting on her eggs? It's fascinating. The hen doesn't move from her position for twenty-one days! I get tired after sitting in the same place for twenty-one minutes! She warms the eggs with her body heat — Hashem makes sure her body heat is the perfect temperature to incubate the eggs. I made sure to bring her food and water, and she sat and she sat and she sat…

Feeding the nesting hen

Every day
she lays
another egg

After waiting for twenty-one days, we were so excited we thought *we* were going to pop. Finally, the eggs hatched twelve adorable yellow chicks.

Our whole family was in awe. The chicks were so tiny. Only a few minutes after they'd hatched, they stood on their two legs and ran around the yard. They jumped around their mother and looked for seeds to eat. Can you imagine a newborn baby running and jumping the moment it's born?

Newborn chicks, just a few hours old!

But enough about our chickens — I still haven't told you anything about the interesting country that I live in — Paraguay.

Paraguay is a country right in the middle of South America, bordered by Bolivia, Argentina, and Brazil. There are only one thousand Jews in all of Paraguay, less than the amount of Jews in some small communities in the United States. My parents came to Paraguay as the Chabad emissaries nine years ago, just before I was born. They came to teach Torah to the Jews of Paraguay. We don't care if there aren't that many Jews in Paraguay; every single Jew is precious!

My father is a *shochet*. He learned how to be a *shochet* before we left for Paraguay, since he knew that there wouldn't be any kosher meat in Paraguay. Without my father, none of the Jews in Paraguay would have kosher meat!

We can't get kosher dairy products in Paraguay either. We bring milk from the village ourselves, and we make sure to watch the milking so that it's *chalav Yisrael*. My mother makes all her own dairy products from this milk.

A neighborhood in Asunción

This morning, when we finished eating breakfast, my father asked us a question.

"Who remembers where we're going today?" he asked.

"To the village to bring milk!" we all shouted excitedly.

"Don't forget that Shavuot is coming," my mother told us. "We need double the usual amount of milk so we can make dairy treats for the holiday."

My stomach was already rumbling, thinking of my mother's cheesecake.

We all love going with my father to get the milk — my older sister, Chana, my younger sisters, Devora, Blumy, and Shayna, and of course, me! Only baby Mendy stays home with my mother — luckily he's too young to know what he's missing.

Before we leave home, we cover ourselves with mosquito repellant. We put it on our arms, our legs, and even on our clothing. There are a lot of mosquitoes in Paraguay. As if mosquito bites aren't bad enough, some of the mosquitoes in Paraguay are poisonous. We never leave the house without mosquito repellant.

Yay! We're going to the village!

On our way to the village, we pass men, women, and even children carrying baskets on their heads. Those baskets are full of chipa, a type of corn bread and a very popular Paraguayan food. I once tried to carry a basket on my head like the Paraguayan children do, but it fell off after five seconds. If you have any balancing tips, please let me know.

Mango and avocado trees grow on the sides of the road. When the mangos and avocados are ripe, they fall to the ground — *plunk!* Beware when walking under a mango or an avocado tree. You don't want an avocado shower, trust me!

Do you want to try carrying this basket on your head?

We stop next to a traffic light, and a bus packed with people stops for us. In Paraguay, you don't have to use the bus stops. You just flag the bus down wherever you want it and it stops for you, like your very own taxi service! But don't get too excited. The buses in Paraguay are so old it's hard to believe they're still riding on the streets. They look like they belong in a museum.

Paraguay has a lot of old-fashioned things. For example, in our backyard there's a well with a metal cover. Many years ago the people who lived in our house didn't have running water. They drew water from the well in our yard. I'm so grateful that we have faucets!

The well in our backyard

A bus in
Paraguay

Our neighborhood is quiet, pleasant, and clean. There are many wealthy people who live here. When we leave our area and drive towards the exit of the city, the scenery changes completely. Instead of nice two-story houses, there are very simple one-story structures. Instead of paved roads, there are dirt roads.

As we get closer to the end of the city, the neighborhood becomes very poor. The roads become harder to travel. The houses on the sides of the roads look like they're about to collapse. Some of them are made from unusual materials like plastic, aluminum, and even cardboard. When it rains, these houses are destroyed and the people must build new ones. The children run through the yards without shoes. They even play soccer barefoot!

I feel very bad for the poor people in Paraguay. When we stop at an intersection, the children stretch their hands out by our car windows, begging for food. We give them cookies and snacks from special boxes that we keep in our car just for them.

Children in the poor neighborhood

Finally, we arrive at the village. From far we can already see Ku-chee-tee, grazing in the yard. Ku-chee-tee is a six-month-old calf whose mother gives us milk. We haven't seen him in so long and he's gotten so big! I run over to him and tug at the rope that's tied around his neck. He follows me down the dirt road towards the house.

Carmen the villager greets us at the door to her house. "*Ola*!" she says, which means "hello" in Spanish. Spanish is one of the official languages of Paraguay. I decide to answer Carmen in her native language, Guarani, the other official language of Paraguay.

"*Baishapa*," I say, which means "hello" in Guarani. "*Heta combi na.*" This means we need a lot of milk. Carmen smiles widely as she listens to me speaking her language.

I only speak a few words of Guarani. At home, we speak Hebrew. I go to virtual school through the computer and we study in English. We speak Spanish with our Jewish neighbors and friends in Paraguay. I speak three different languages every day — four if you count chicken language.

You grew so much, Ku-chee-tee!

Carmen sits near the cow and begins to milk her. My father watches the milking while we all stand on the side and watch the pails practically overflow with milk. Well, we did ask for a lot of milk! Then Carmen lets me milk the cow by myself for the very first time. It's fun, but much harder than I thought it would be. I'm glad I don't have to do it every day. I'd rather go to school.

Motti milks a cow

We pour the milk into the buckets we brought from home and my father pays Carmen.

"*Muchas gracias*," we say, which means "thank you very much" in Spanish. She walks us to the exit and she waves goodbye to my little sister Shayna. I only wish we could take Ku-chee-tee home with us.

Now that's a lot of milk!

We don't pass any parks or playgrounds on the way home. That's because there aren't any in our city! But there are other nice places we can go to relax. For example, there's a pretty lake not far from our house. Sometimes we rent a boat there, and we sail along the riverbanks.

Looking at the horizon

Have you ever driven a car? I have, and I've driven on a real road, too! At special times the municipality of Asunción closes the roads to regular cars. Instead, the cars are only open to special cars that are driven by children. I love taking my sisters for long rides. I feel like I'm driving a real car.

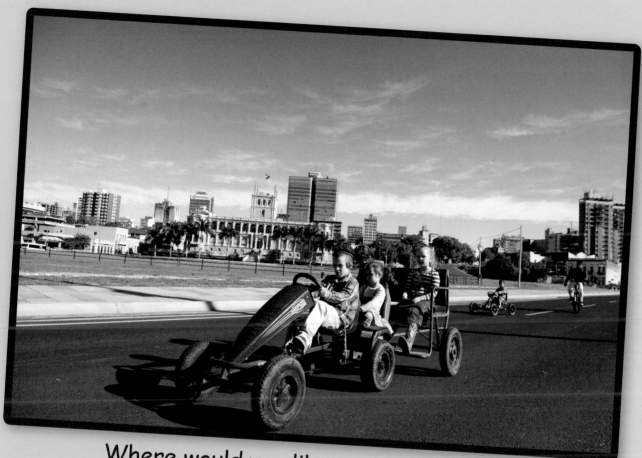

Where would you like to drive today?

Ahhhh. We're home. We help my father lug the fresh milk into the kitchen.

"Good job!" my mother says as she comes to greet us. "You brought home lots of milk. Now we can make delicious things for Shavuot."

I love the holiday of Shavuot. We make all sorts of dairy dishes like cheesecake, yogurt, and ice cream. Remember, I can't buy kosher ice cream in the store. Ice cream is a humongous treat!

My mother transfers the milk from the buckets to pots, which she heats on the stovetop. She is pasteurizing the milk — this kills all of the harmful bacteria in it.

Now that the milk is safe to eat, we can make cheese from it. We squeeze a bit of lemon juice into the pot of milk and wait for the curds to separate from the milk. The curds look like fluffy clouds.

When we see that the milk has formed cheese, we transfer it to a clean cloth. We hang the cloth up overnight and all of the liquid drains out of it, leaving delicious cheese inside!

Be patient.
We'll have
cheese
tomorrow.

In the afternoon we gather in our Chabad House for our Tzivos Hashem activity. My mother, sisters, and I bring all of the materials we need.

The Chabad House also houses the synagogue. It's where we daven and celebrate events, and it's where my parents give Torah lectures to adults and children.

During davening, I always greet the congregants and help them find the right place in their siddur. When my father is away, I also need to daven out loud so that people can follow the services. But I'll tell you a secret — I'm shy, and davening out loud in front of everyone makes me a little bit uncomfortable.

When my father's away, there's nobody else to do it but me. So I take a deep breath and do it.

My mother once told me that it makes her feel so proud when she hears me sing *Lechah Dodi* out loud just like my father does. She knows it isn't easy for me to do it, which makes her even prouder.

Asunción Jewish Kids Club

The activities at the Chabad House take place on Sunday, which is our day off from school. Jewish children from Asunción come to learn about the Jewish holidays, to learn Torah, and to hear stories of righteous Jews. The Chabad House is also the place that I meet my friends. All of my friends in Asunción are younger than me, so I feel a little bit like their counselor. My only friends who are my age are my classmates, but I only get to see them on the computer. It's pretty hard to play ball over a computer screen! Sometimes I think, *Wouldn't it be nice to have a Jewish friend my age in Asunción?* But usually, I'm happy to play with my younger friends.

Hello, *amigos*!

"*Ola!*" we say to the parents who arrive at the Chabad House.

"*Keh-tah* (What's new)?" they answer us. My friend Meir's father arrives holding his *guampa*. A *guampa* sounds like an animal, doesn't it? It's actually an ox's horn, filled with the most popular drink in Paraguay, *terere*. *Terere* is made by filling the *guampa* with assorted leaves and ice water. The leaves flavor the cold water just like tea bags flavor hot water. *Terere* is drunk through a metal straw that has a filter on it to make sure you don't accidentally drink the leaves.

In Paraguay, you don't leave home without your *guampa*. People take it with them to work, on trips, and when they go out with friends. They even bring it to the shul with them when they come to hear Torah classes!

"Meir's really excited to see you," Meir's mother tells me. I hurry inside to look for my friend.

This is how you fill a *guampa* with *terere*

Meir's father with his *guampa*

The children sit in a circle and my mother tells them all about the holiday of Shavuot. She tells them about Har Sinai and about the Torah that was given to the Jews on this special day.

Every activity in the Chabad House includes some sort of project. Who doesn't love doing a project — especially one that you can eat?

Today, we make a sweet Har Sinai. My mother baked a lot of cupcakes in advance, and each kid receives their own little cupcakes shaped like a mountain. Then she gives them candies to decorate their cupcake with. My sisters and I help to make sure that the little kids don't ruin their cupcakes — or eat the decorations!

When they're done, each child puts their cupcake onto a plate — now they each have their very own Har Sinai!

A delicious Har Sinai

Then my mother brings all of the children to the shul where my father is waiting for them. He tells them all about the holy Torah that we received on Har Sinai and how Hashem chose the children specifically to be responsible for taking care of the Torah and the mitzvot. The children promised to keep the Torah and to pass it along from generation to generation. It was in the merit of the children that *Am Yisrael* got the Torah. What a privilege!

My father opens up the *aron kodesh* and shows the children the Torah scrolls inside.

"On Shavuot," my father says, "the Lubavitcher Rebbe encouraged every girl and boy to come to shul and hear the Ten Commandments that Hashem gave us on Har Sinai."

I can see the excitement in the children's eyes.

"Rabino Levi," asks a little boy named Moshe, "can the little children come too?"

Rabino means "rabbi" in Spanish. That is what the children call my father.

"Of course, Moshe," Rabino answers, meaning, my father. "The Torah is for every single Jew!"

Rabino, we want to kiss the *sefer Torah*, too!

Unfortunately, it's time for the activities to end. The children's parents are already waiting outside to pick them up and bring them home. Moshe, David, Chana, and all of the children say good-bye.

I look at all of the children as they leave. David, who just received a Jewish name a month ago; Moshe, who started keeping kosher this year; and Meir, who already knows how to read Hebrew. This is why we were sent by the Lubavitcher Rebbe to Paraguay — for David and for Moshe and for Meir, for their parents and for all of the Jews in Paraguay.

I love my friends

While I was busy thinking, my father sat down to learn Torah. I sat next to him and he looked at me and smiled.

"Abba," I said, "we're so lucky. The children were chosen specifically to take care of the Torah and to pass it along from one generation to the next. And we were chosen specifically to come to Paraguay to teach the Jews here Torah so that they can pass it along to the next generation."

My father looked at me. It was a look full of emotion, happiness, and so much love.

I might be far from all of my cousins. I might not have any friends my age. I can't buy cheese in the grocery store and I don't even have a park to play in. But would I give up the privilege of bringing Torah to the Jews of Paraguay for any of those things? Not a chance!

Abba, we are so lucky to be here

Now how do you like that?

Fascinating Facts about Paraguay

Paraguay is a medium-sized country in South America. It is bordered by Argentina, Bolivia, and Brazil.

Paraguay is located in the Southern Hemisphere, below the equator. That means its seasons are the opposite of those in the United States. When it's winter in the U.S., it's summer in Paraguay, and vice versa!

The Paraguay River is very long — 1,629 miles! It passes through Brazil, Bolivia, Paraguay, and Argentina. The river crosses Paraguay from north to south.

The Parana River runs through the center of the South American continent. It passes through Brazil, Paraguay, and Argentina. The word *Parana* comes from the ancient Tupi language that was spoken in Brazil many years ago. It means "as big as the sea."

Tens of years ago, there were eighteen beautiful waterfalls on the Parana River. They were the mightiest waterfalls in the world. The sound of those falls could be heard from nearly twenty miles away — about the distance from Queens to Manhattan! A giant dam that was built flooded those falls and they disappeared forever. Today, there is only one tiny fall left over from that spectacular wonder.

Paraguay was discovered about five hundred years ago by Sebastian Cabot as he sailed down the Paraguay and Parana rivers.

Paraguay is home to many forms of unusual wildlife. Some of these include the giant anteater and a variety of rare snakes and birds.

The average length of a giant anteater is 6 feet, 6 inches, longer than most men! They live in the rainforests and spend most of their time searching for food. Their favorite food is — you guessed it — ants! The giant anteater can eat thirty thousand ants per day and a few thousand ants in only one minute!

The Native Americans were the first people to settle in Paraguay. They spoke Guarani, one of the official languages of Paraguay. Most Paraguayans speak Guarani. It is the most commonly spoken language in the villages of Paraguay.

Most of Paraguay's population lives close to the capital of Asunción.

One-third to one-half of Paraguay's population is poor. There are big gaps between the rich and the poor. In the center of the city there are beautiful, tall buildings, and in the poorer areas people live in huts that are destroyed every time it rains.

Terere is the national drink of Paraguay; it's a cold drink based on leaves.

Peddlers sell leaves for making terere on every street corner. Paraguayans drink many quarts of terere every day from their guampas — special flasks made from ox horns.

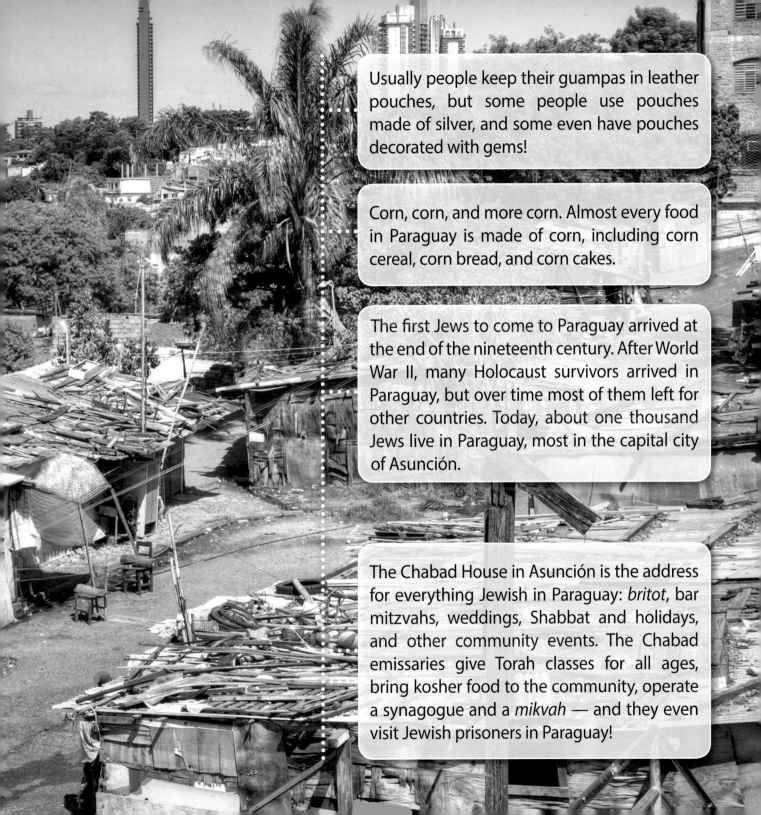

Usually people keep their guampas in leather pouches, but some people use pouches made of silver, and some even have pouches decorated with gems!

Corn, corn, and more corn. Almost every food in Paraguay is made of corn, including corn cereal, corn bread, and corn cakes.

The first Jews to come to Paraguay arrived at the end of the nineteenth century. After World War II, many Holocaust survivors arrived in Paraguay, but over time most of them left for other countries. Today, about one thousand Jews live in Paraguay, most in the capital city of Asunción.

The Chabad House in Asunción is the address for everything Jewish in Paraguay: *britot*, bar mitzvahs, weddings, Shabbat and holidays, and other community events. The Chabad emissaries give Torah classes for all ages, bring kosher food to the community, operate a synagogue and a *mikvah* — and they even visit Jewish prisoners in Paraguay!

The Recycled Orchestra

The people of Paraguay love to play and to listen to music. Many of Paraguay's poor have no way of buying instruments. Instead, they create their own instruments from scraps they find. For example, a violin or a cello can be crafted from an empty oil barrel. A flute can be made from tubing and spoons, and an empty crate can create a lovely guitar. When all of these instruments are played together, you have a recycled orchestra!

Make Your Own Instrument

A Homemade Panpipe

Materials Needed

- 8 drinking straws
- scissors
- a ruler
- colorful Scotch tape
- a dark marker

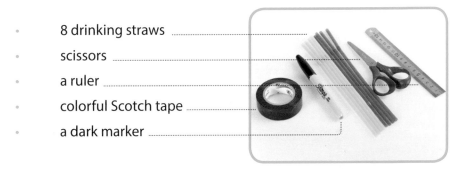

What to Do

1 Cut the drinking straws to the following lengths and write the coordinating number on each straw.

3.7 inches	3.9 inches	4.5 inches	5.1 inches	5.7 inches	6.1 inches	6.7 inches	7.7 inches
1	2	3	4	5	6	7	8

2 Arrange the numbered straws from shortest to longest. You can put pieces of straw (about .7 inches each) in between each of the numbered straws (from the pieces that you cut).

3 Attach the straws with a strip of colorful tape.
Your panpipe is ready!
Now you can play a tune.

Blow into your numbered straws according to this set of numbers.
Do you know this song?

3212333 222 355   3212333 322321

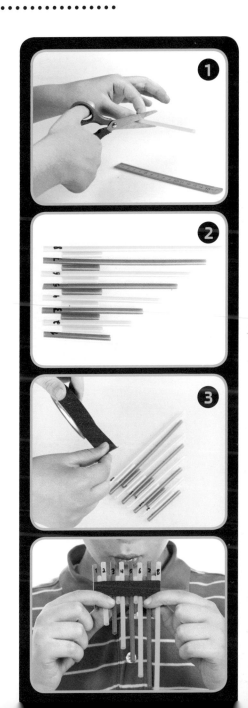

Say It in Spanish!

Hello - Ola

How are you? - Cómo está usted?

Please - Por favor

Thank you - Gracias

Mother - Mama

Father - Papa

Boy - Nino

Girl - Nina

Friend - Amigo (male)

Friend - Amiga (female)

Game - Juego

Book - Libro

Car - Coche